GERSHWIN
TRANSCRIPTIONS FOR PIANO
18 Song Hits Arranged by the Composer

EDITED BY MAURICE HINSON

AN ALFRED MASTERWORK EDITION

Cover art: Portrait of George Gershwin *(1898–1937)*
by Arthur Kaufman (1888–1971)
Oil on canvas board (15 3/4 x 11 3/4 in.)
National Portrait Gallery, Smithsonian Institution
Art Resource, NY

GEORGE GERSHWIN®

Contents

This collection is dedicated to Joanne Haroutounian,
with appreciation and admiration.

Maurice Hinson

Transcriptions for Piano
18 Song Hits Arranged by the Composer
Edited by Maurice Hinson

Foreword

George Gershwin (1898–1937) was one of the most imaginative American composers of the 1920s and '30s. He fused elements of jazz with European symphonic tradition. His major works that combined both traditions, such as *Rhapsody in Blue, Concerto in F, An American in Paris* and *Porgy and Bess*, display a rich and diversified style that is completely and unmistakably American. Upon first hearing Gershwin, audiences went wild with enthusiasm and agreed that here was a fresh, brilliant talent with a great future. This editor grew up playing and singing Gershwin's music, and is delighted to be able to share the wonderful gems included in this collection.

Gershwin as Composer

George Gershwin grew up in Brooklyn, New York as part of a Russian immigrant family. His parents, Moshe and Rose Gershovitz, had come to the United States in the 1890s. Neither of his parents was musical; however, George found a fellow artist in his older brother Ira, who wrote many of the lyrics for his songs.

After the Gershwins bought a piano in 1912, George began studying with neighborhood teachers. He later studied with Rubin Goldmark (1872–1936), Wallingford Riegger (1885–1961), Henry Cowell (1897–1965), Joseph Schillinger (1895–1943) and Edward Kilenyi (1884–1968). At the age of 15, George was hired by the music publishing firm Jerome H. Remick & Co. as a "song plugger"—a pianist who played and sang songs for prospective customers. He made his first piano rolls in 1915 and began composing piano pieces. He also composed musical comedies, which were very successful. George later experimented with jazz and popular idioms, and he incorporated these types of music into his orchestral compositions. His major works include *Rhapsody in Blue* (1924), *Concerto in F* (1925), *An American in Paris* (1928) and the American folk opera *Porgy and Bess* (1935). In 1932, Gershwin created wonderful piano arrangements of 18 of his song hits, all of which are included in this collection.

Gershwin was one of the most gifted American composers in terms of pure native talent. Out of the elements of jazz, ragtime and blues, he created a musical language that was fresh, spontaneous and, above all, American. Soon after the first season of *Porgy and Bess*, Gershwin became ill. He was only 39 years old when he died in 1937 of a brain hemorrhage.

Gershwin as Pianist

Gershwin's first neighborhood piano teacher was Charles Hamblitzer, who introduced his young student to the works of Chopin, Liszt and Debussy. However, as a young man, George became vitally associated with the popular songwriting and publishing industry known as Tin Pan Alley, when he was hired to promote popular songs by playing and singing them for performers looking for new music. After breaking away from Tin Pan Alley, Gershwin gained recognition for his public performances, and cut over 100 piano rolls. According to Wyatt, "He expounded the rhythmic subtleties of the jazz numbers brilliantly and with exactly the proper atmosphere of impromptu that makes good jazz playing so fascinating."[1] Gershwin also became a very skilled vocal accompanist. He worked as a rehearsal pianist and composed full scores for numerous Broadway shows and productions.

In 1924, Gershwin composed and performed his *Rhapsody in Blue* for piano and orchestra with Paul Whiteman and his band. This work had overwhelming success and brought jazz directly into the concert hall.

Performing Gershwin's Piano Pieces

Gershwin gave the following advice about playing popular music at the piano, including his own works:

> *To play American popular music most effectively, one must guard against the natural tendency to make too frequent use of the sustaining [damper] pedal. Our study of the great Romantic composers has trained us in the method of the legato, whereas our popular music asks for staccato effects, for almost a stenciled style. The rhythms of American popular music are more or less brittle; they should be made to snap, and at times to crackle. The more sharply the music is played, the more effective it sounds. Most pianists with a classical training fail lamentably in the playing of our ragtime or jazz because they use the pedaling of Chopin when interpreting the blues of Handy. The Romantic touch is very good in a sentimental ballad, but in a tune of strict rhythm, it is somewhat out of place.[2]*

---

[1] Robert Wyatt, "The Seven Jazz Preludes of George Gershwin: A Historical Narrative." *American Music*, Vol. 7, No. 4, Spring 1989, pp. 70–71.

[2] *Gershwin at the Keyboard.* New York: no date. Introduction by George Gershwin. Inside front cover.

Gershwin flourished during a period of time when jazz rhythms were popular. Eighth notes were frequently played with a swing rhythm: ♫ = ♩♪. In performing Gershwin's piano pieces, look for places where this rhythmic flexibility may be used.

About Gershwin's Song Transcriptions

Gershwin created these 18 song transcriptions between 1919 and 1931 and played them at numerous private parties, often with many variations. His impromptu performances served as the basis for these solo piano transcriptions. In these pieces, one can detect Gershwin's unique playing style, which was influenced by Mike Bernard, Les Copeland, Melville Ellis, Lucky Roberts, and Zez Confrey, among others.

About This Edition

All fingerings, pedal indications and metronome marks are editorial, unless otherwise indicated. All parenthetical material is editorial. This edition is based on *Gershwin at the Keyboard*, New World Music Corp., New York, no date.

Acknowledgements

Thanks to editors E. L. Lancaster, Carol Matz and Sharon Aaronson for their generous assistance and expert editorial advice, and to Brandi Lowe for her superb administrative assistance.

Suggested Further Reading

Kilenyi, Edward, Sr. "George Gershwin As I Knew Him," *The Etude* (1950), 11.

Levine, Henry. "Gershwin, Handy and the Blues," *Clavier*, IX/7 (1970), 10.

Rimler, Walter. *A Gershwin Companion: A Critical Inventory and Discography, 1916–1984*, Ann Arbor, MI: Popular Culture, 1991.

About the Music

Clap Yo' Hands 6

This song was composed in 1926 for the musical comedy *Oh, Kay!* In measures 3–4, 11–12, etc., arpeggiate the large chords by beginning the lower notes slightly before the beat and playing the top note on the beat.

Form: **A** = measures 1–16; **B** = 17–24; **A**¹ = 25–32.

Source: *Gershwin at the Keyboard*. New World Music Corp., New York, no date. (This piece is one of 18 song hits that Gershwin arranged for piano. Other pieces in this collection, with this same source listed, were also song hits arranged by Gershwin.)

Do-Do-Do. 8

This song was composed by George and Ira Gershwin in only thirty minutes. It was written for the musical comedy *Oh, Kay!*, which was introduced at the Imperial Theater in New York City on November 8, 1926.

Form: **A** = measures 1–8; **B** = 9–24; **B**¹ = 25–31; codetta = 31-32.

Do It Again. 10

This song was composed in 1922 for the musical comedy *The French Doll*. Bring out the tenor voice in measures 1–4, 17–19 and 29–32.

Form: **A** = measures 1–16 (Part I = 1–8, Part II = 9–16); **A**¹ = 17–32.

Source: *Gershwin at the Keyboard*. New World Music Corp., New York, no date.

Fascinating Rhythm 12

Composed in 1924, this song was written for the musical comedy *Lady, Be Good!* Keep the left-hand eighth notes in measures 1–10 steady, under the highly syncopated right-hand melody. Use *poco rubato* at measures 16 and 29.

Form: Introduction = measures 1–2; **A** = 3–18; **A**¹ = 19–34.

Source: *Gershwin at the Keyboard*. New World Music Corp., New York, no date.

I Got Rhythm 14

Composed in 1928, originally in a slower tempo, Gershwin used this song as the basis of his *I Got Rhythm Variations* for piano and orchestra (1934). The main theme is built on the major pentatonic scale.

Form: **A** = measures 1–16; **B** = 17–25; **A**¹ = 25–34; bridge = 35–38; **A**¹ = 39–54; **B**¹ = 54–62; **A**² = 63–72.

I'll Build a Stairway to Paradise 18

This piece was written in 1922 for the annual Broadway review *George White's Scandals*. Beginning in 1920, Gershwin wrote the music for *George White's Scandals* for five consecutive years. This was one of the most popular songs from that series.

Form: **A** = measures 1–12; **A**¹ = 13–18.

Source: *Gershwin at the Keyboard*. New World Music Corp., New York, no date.

Liza (All the Clouds'll Roll Away) 44

This 1929 composition was conceived as a big minstrel number for the musical *Show Girl*. The piece opens in a leisurely pace with a swinging beat that is retained throughout.

Form: **A** = measures 1–16; **B** = 17–24; **A**¹ = 24–32; **A**² = 33–48; **B**¹ = 49–56; **A**³ = 57–64.

This song was composed in 1924 but did not make it into a musical until 1927, when it appeared in the musical comedy *Strike Up the Band*. The transcription for solo piano appeared in *George Gershwin's Songbook* (1932).

Form: **A** = measures 1–16; **B** = 17–24; **A** = 25–32; codetta = 32–33.

Source: *Gershwin at the Keyboard*. New World Music Corp., New York, no date.

This song was composed in 1927 for the Broadway musical *Funny Face*, starring Fred Astaire and Gertrude McDonald. Arpeggiated minor tenths are frequently used. Major and minor harmonies are juxtaposed at measures 23–24, with a staccato touch. Be sure to release the pedal in measure 32 exactly on beat three, so that the final B-flat octave sounds clear as a bell, but quiet.

Form: **A** = measures 1–8; **A**^{1} = 9–16; **B** = 17–24; **A**^{2} = 25–32.

This song was composed between 1914 and 1917 while Gershwin was "plugging" songs for the Remick Music Company in New York. Gershwin made a piano roll of this piece in October, 1919.

Form: **A** = measures 1–8; **B** = 9–16; **A**^{1} = 17–24; **C** = 25–32.

This song was composed in 1924 for the Broadway musical of the same title. On December 4, 1925, Gershwin accompanied contralto Marguerite d'Alvarez as she performed this song at the Roosevelt Hotel in New York City.

Form: **A** = measures 1–8; **A**^{1} = 9–16; **B** = 17–24; **A**^{2} = 25–32.

This song was written for *George White's Scandals* of 1924. Bring out the left-hand melody in measures 1–2, 7–10, 15–16 and 25–26. Play the final chord in measure 32 abruptly, and release it immediately.

Form: Introduction = measures 1–2; **A** = 3–16; **B** = 17–24; **A**^{1} = 25–30; codetta = 31–32.

Source: *Gershwin at the Keyboard*. New World Music Corp., New York, no date.

Composed in 1927, this piece was introduced in the Broadway musical of the same name on September 5, 1927. The lyrics were originally anti-war (referring to World War I), but in 1940, with America involved in World War II, Ira Gershwin changed the lyrics to be more appropriate for the times.

Form: Introduction = measures 1–2; **A** = 3–17; transition = 17–18; **B** = 19–26; **A**^{1} = 26–36.

Gershwin composed this big hit in 1919. When Al Jolson used it in his show *Sinbad*, it became extremely popular. Notice the melodic reference to Stephen Foster's song *Old Folks at Home* ("Way down upon the Swanee River…") at measures 32–33.

Form: **A** = measures 1–16; **A**^{1} = 17–31; codetta 31–32.

Source: *Gershwin at the Keyboard*. New World Music Corp., New York, no date.

This song was composed in 1925 for the Broadway musical *Tip-Toes*. The title is a play on the old song "Sweet and Low."

Form: **A** = measures 1–8; **A**^{1} = 9–16; **B** = 17–24; **A**^{1} = 25–32.

George's brother Ira Gershwin wrote the lyrics for this 1927 song. The piano transcription came out in *George Gershwin's Songbook* (1932).

Form: **A** = measures 1–16; **B** = 17–24; **A**^{1} = 25–31; codetta 31–32.

Source: *Gershwin at the Keyboard*. New World Music Corp., New York, no date.

Composed in 1925 for the Broadway musical *Tip-Toes*, this song provided the title for the 1956 Bob Hope movie (which also featured Eva Marie Saint and Pearl Bailey). Gershwin recorded two piano rolls of this piece in 1926.

Form: Introduction = measure 1; **A** = 2–14; **A**^{1} = 15–25; **A**^{2} = 26–31; codetta = 32–35.

This song was written in 1931 for the Broadway musical *Of Thee I Sing*. The piece features an angular bass line, which gives it an unsettling feeling.

Form: **A** = measures 1–17; **A**^{1} = 18–24; coda = 25–32.

Clap Yo' Hands

Music and Lyrics by
George Gershwin and Ira Gershwin

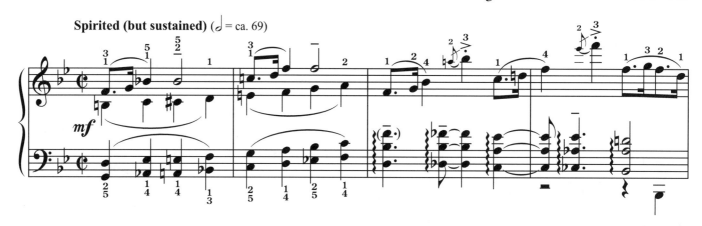

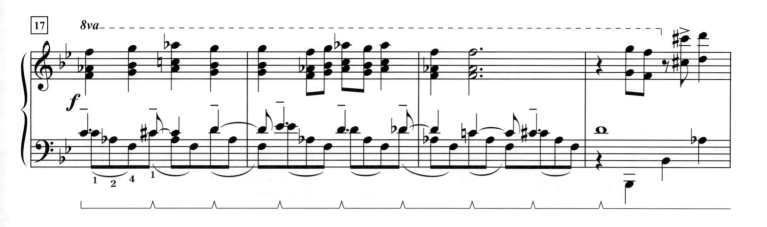

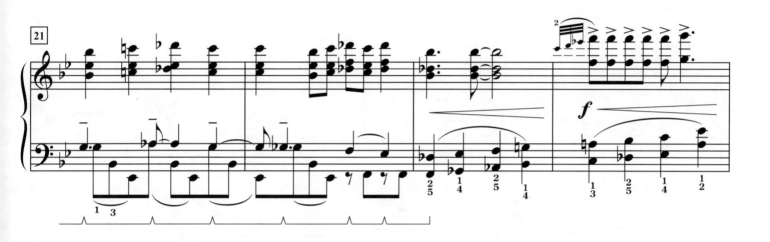

Do-Do-Do

Music and Lyrics by
George Gershwin and Ira Gershwin

In a swinging manner (♩ = ca. 69)

Do It Again

Music by George Gershwin
Lyrics by B.G. DeSylva

(a) Play the notes in small type very quietly.

Fascinating Rhythm

Music and Lyrics by
George Gershwin and Ira Gershwin

I Got Rhythm

Music and Lyrics by
George Gershwin and Ira Gershwin

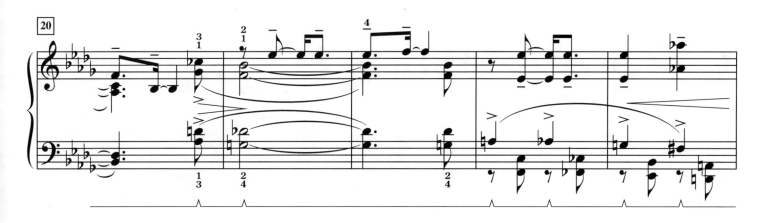

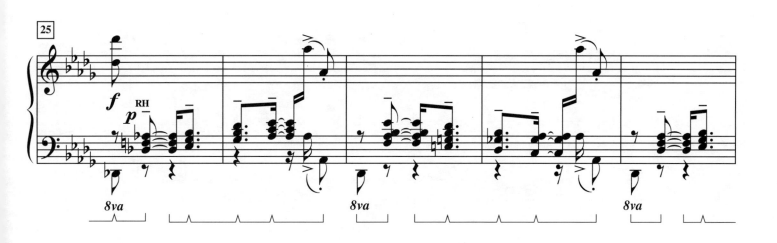

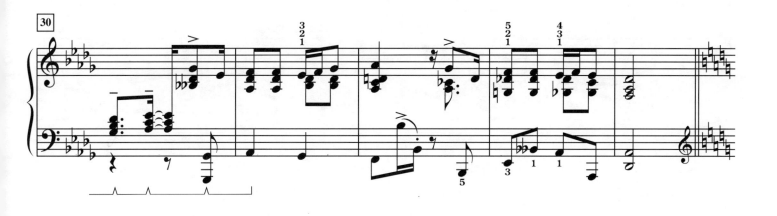

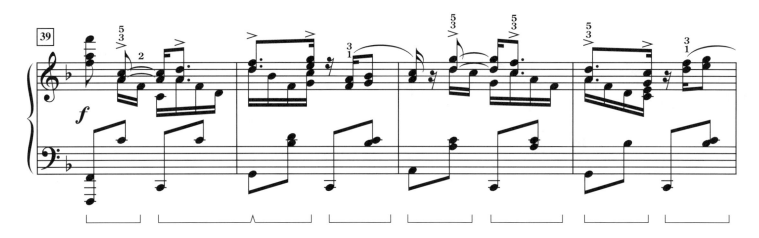

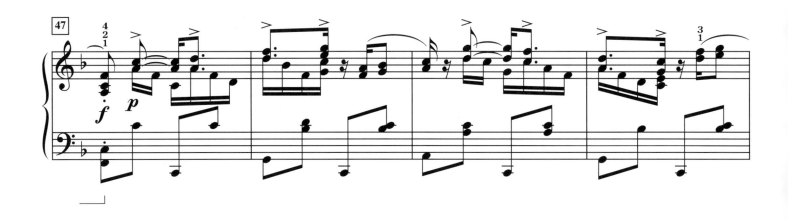

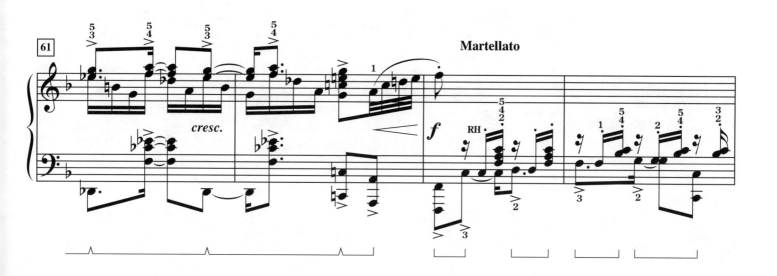

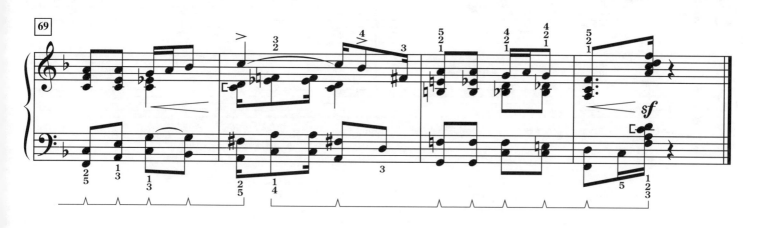

I'll Build a Stairway to Paradise

Music by George Gershwin
Lyrics by B.G. DeSylva and Ira Gershwin

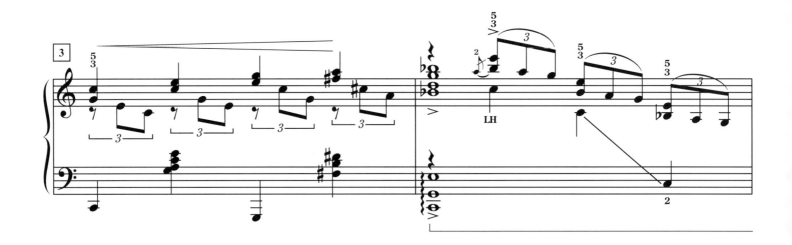

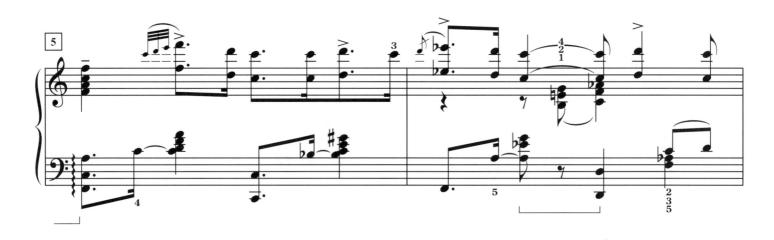

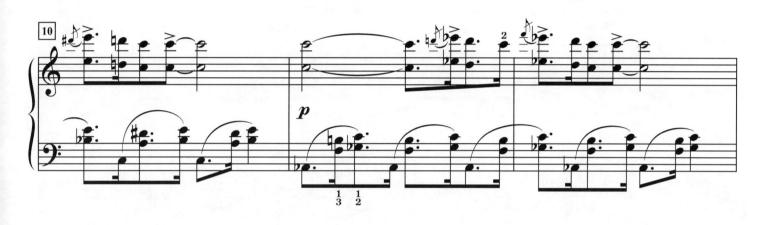

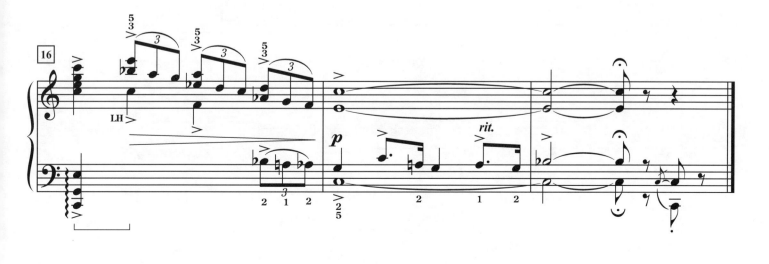

The Man I Love

Music and Lyrics by
George Gershwin and Ira Gershwin

Slow and in a singing style (♩ = ca. 66)

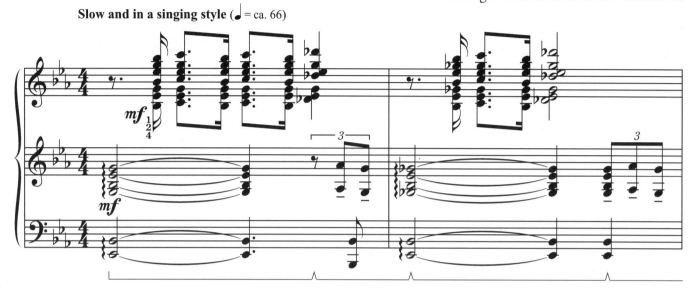

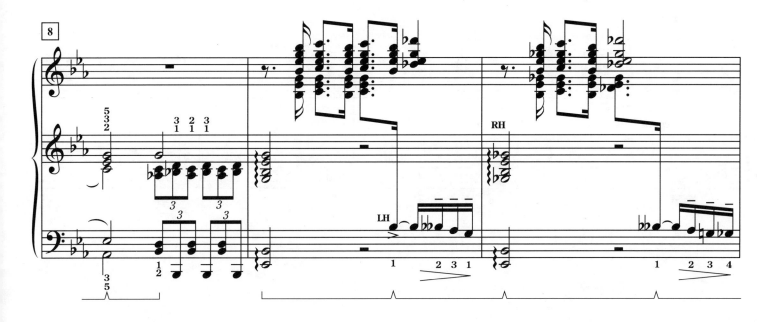

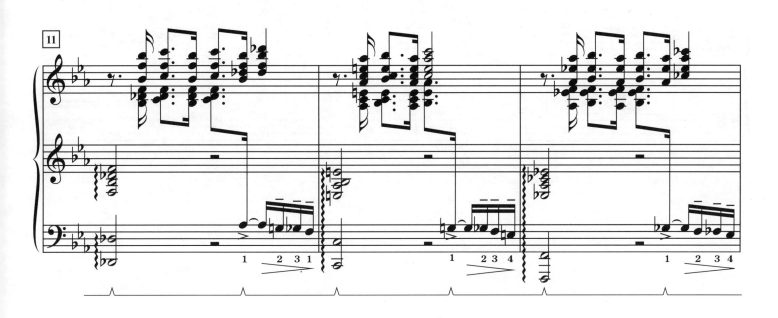

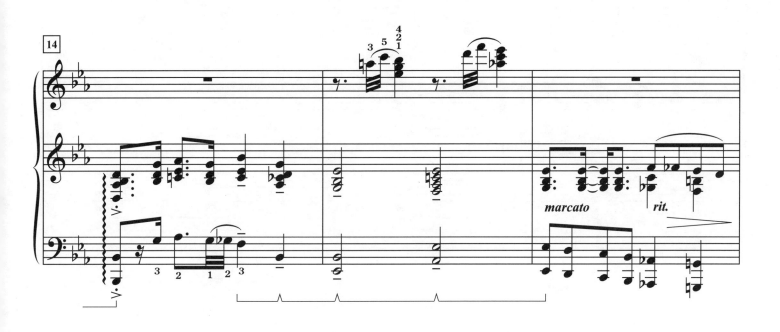

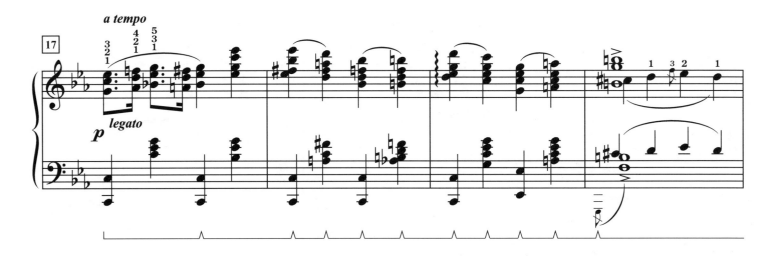

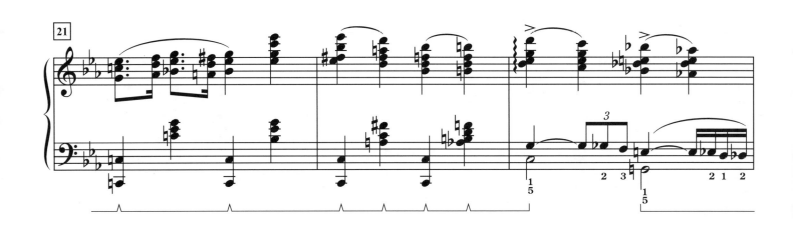

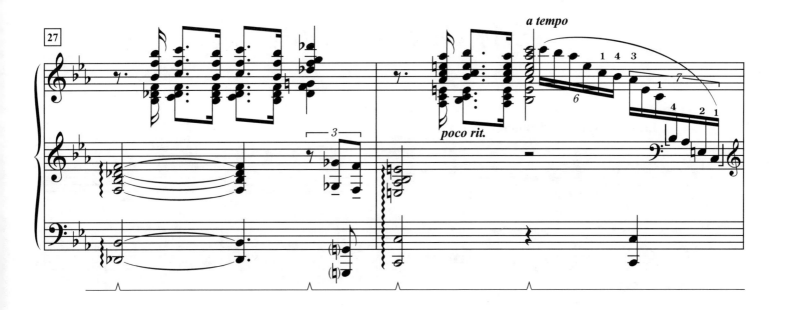

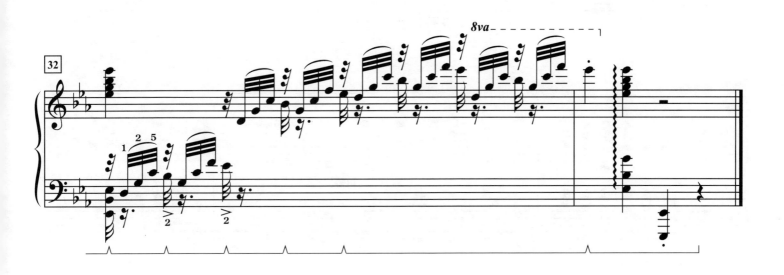

My One and Only

Music and Lyrics by
George Gershwin and Ira Gershwin

Lively, in a strong rhythm (♩ = ca. 66)

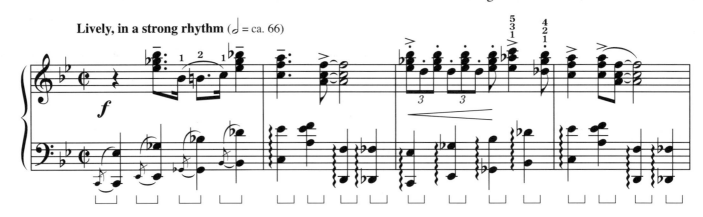

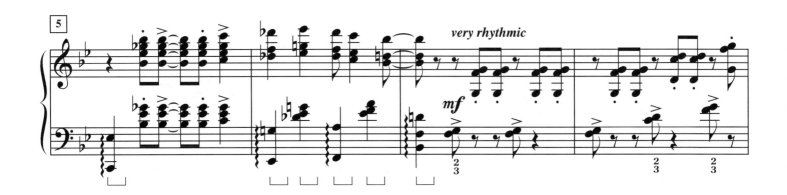

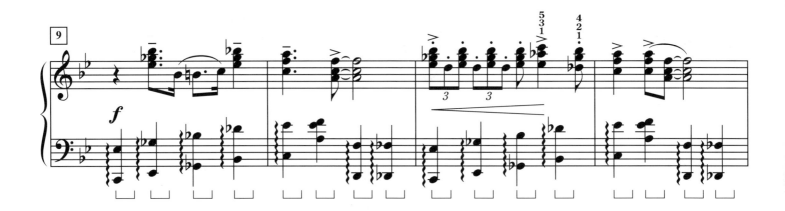

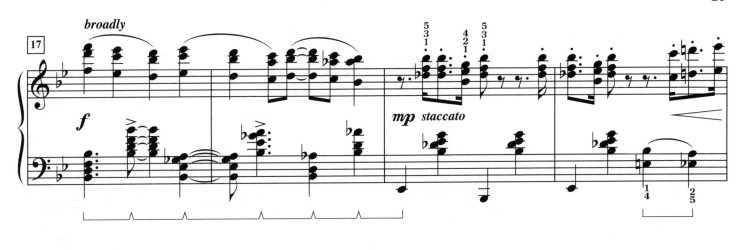

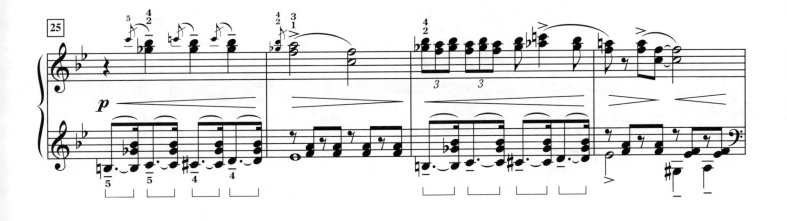

Nobody But You

Music by George Gershwin
Lyrics by B.G. DeSylva and Arthur Jackson

Oh, Lady Be Good

Music and Lyrics by
George Gershwin and Ira Gershwin

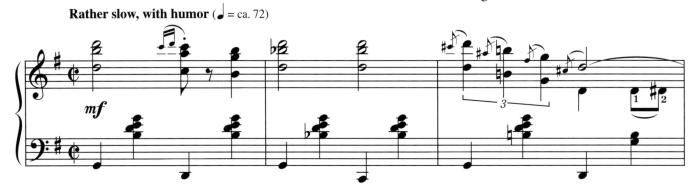

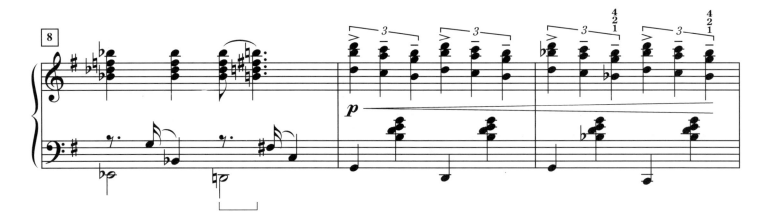

Somebody Loves Me

Music by George Gershwin
Lyrics by B.G. DeSylva
and Ballard Macdonald

Strike Up the Band

Music and Lyrics by
George Gershwin and Ira Gershwin

Swanee

Music by George Gershwin
Lyrics by Irving Caesar

Sweet and Low Down

Music and Lyrics by
George Gershwin and Ira Gershwin

'S Wonderful

Music and Lyrics by
George Gershwin and Ira Gershwin

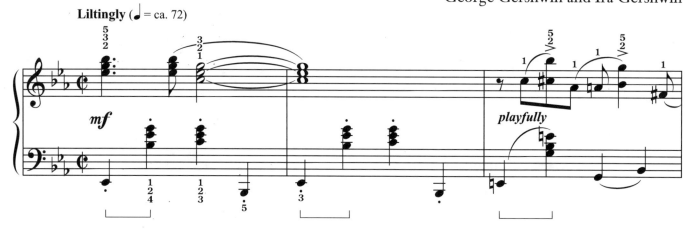

That Certain Feeling

Music and Lyrics by
George Gershwin and Ira Gershwin

Ardently (♩ = ca. 63)

Who Cares?
(So Long As You Care for Me)

Music and Lyrics by
George Gershwin and Ira Gershwin

Liza
(All the Clouds'll Roll Away)

Music by George Gershwin
Lyrics by Ira Gershwin and Gus Kahn